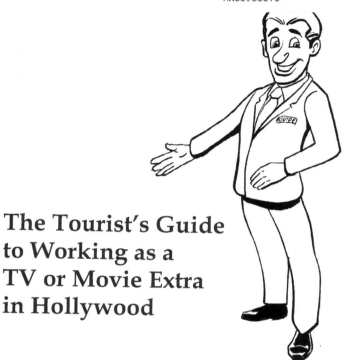

The Tourist's Guide to Working as a TV or Movie Extra in Hollywood

Darryl Stewart

with Kimberly Kimmel and
Elda Minger

© Illustrations by Arne Starr

Published by Profitable Stewardship, Inc. We are not responsible for the content, nor do we own any rights to this publication.

Dedication

I need to thank my late mother,

Maggie Stewart,

for instilling in me my creative motivation.

She taught me how to implement ideas

and see them through.

I want to thank my twin daughters,

Chanel and Jhanel Stewart.

You are the light of my life.

I'm writing this book for both of you.

Finally, I'd like to thank my close friend,

Melissa Culiner,

for her encouragement,

and valuable input which helped me

complete this book,

and for keeping me healthy.

Disclaimer

This book is solely created to aid in the information and edification to those individuals who wish to seek out employment as an extra while visiting Los Angeles. While the author and publisher (we) want to inform and make our information an enjoyable read, we, in no way guarantee, suggest, or make any assurance to anyone who reads this book that any type of employment as an extra in the entertainment industry can be obtained, whether on a full or part-time basis. Many factors come into play when exploring any type of employment in the entertainment industry. We can offer absolutely no guarantee you will achieve the results you seek.

We will not provide counseling in any form. The author of this book is merely sharing his own experiences and research of his professional years as an extra while working in the entertainment industry. This book is intended to inspire you toward your personal goal of becoming knowledgeable and seeking out employment in the field of extra work. Please feel free to read any books on the topic of getting work in the entertainment industry that you feel will help you learn additional information.

No liability or responsibility of any kind will be made against the author or publisher with respect to any damages or loss that might be experienced by any reader, whether directly or indirectly, due to the use of information contained within this book.

About Darryl

In the mid 1990's, I was in an online chat room when someone asked, "What's going on with that TV show you're working on?" I began to be blasted with more show business questions like: "How can I get into the acting business?", "What do I need to do to get on a Hollywood set?", "Can I get an autograph?", "How can I come out to Los Angeles and be an extra?" I instantly realized there were tons of people out there who wanted to learn how to get into the acting business.

People in the chat room who lived outside of Los Angeles seemed especially interested in coming to Hollywood to check out the possibilities of working and rubbing elbows with film and TV stars while on vacation.

Over the next few years, I tossed around several ideas in my mind. I asked my acting co-workers what they thought about a book written for people who were on vacation in Los Angeles and wanted to work as an extra or background actor on a TV or movie set. Everyone thought it was a great idea!

I never planned to get into the acting business. The opportunity came to me. I was born and raised in Los Angeles. One day, after school, in the middle of a basketball practice, the father of one of the cheerleaders walked over to a group of kids standing with the cheerleaders about 500 feet away from me on the field. He appeared to ask them something. I couldn't hear them, but all of a sudden, they all looked at me and pointed. (Seventh grade can be rough enough without a bunch of girls pointing at you). The man began to walk toward me. As he approached, I became nervous.

"Just keep shooting," he said. I answered, "Okay." After which we chatted for a few minutes. He turned back to the girls and they gave him a thumbs up sign.

I asked, "What's going on here?" That's when he asked me if I ever thought about doing commercials. He was looking to cast an African-American.

He wound up casting me in my first commercial because I didn't sound ethnic and I could bounce two basketballs at the same time. That was how it started for me; being in the right place, at the right time.

I shot several commercials as a youth and really enjoyed it. I started acting at 11 years old. I always loved being on set and felt very comfortable in that environment. As an adult, I got into the background acting business because I was laid off from a corporate job. That was when I decided to sign-up and do it as a profession.

I've now been a background actor for over 20 years and have worked on numerous major TV shows, blockbuster movies, national commercials, as well as big budget music videos.

In my career, I've had the opportunity to meet numerous interesting people who have decided to be background actors themselves. Within the extra and background community, there are many people from all walks of life, ranging from Desert Storm veterans to athletes who played in the NFL Super Bowl. Meeting and working with these people has given me memories I will cherish forever.

Signing up to be a background actor was one of the best decisions I've made. In my two-decade career, I've had the time of my life and don't regret one minute being on a set or location shoot. I've been able to see how television shows are shot, how a movie is put together from start to finish, and I've had the pleasure of meeting many famous actors, directors, and producers and consider a lot of them familiar acquaintances.

Does this sound exciting? You bet it does!

If you'd like to earn money while actually working with stars and experience the thrill of being on a real television or movie set, this book is for you. See you on set!

Darryl D. Stewart

Table of Contents

Connect with us:

www.Facebook.com/beanextraonvacation

https://twitter.com/touristguide14

www.darryldstewart.com

Introduction

Why only go on a tour of a Hollywood studio to see stars when you can walk right on a set and work with the actors yourself? While on your vacation in Los Angeles, instead of simply taking a studio tour, why not be directly involved in the making of television shows and movies?

When tourists come to Los Angeles they want to see somebody famous. They typically pay for tours to stars' homes. They rarely see anyone famous, even if they go on a tour of a studio. Some tourists want to discover how a television show or movie is made.

How many tourists have the opportunity to actually work with the stars? In this book, I'm going to tell you how you can do just that, work side by side with television and movie actors, and how easy the process can actually be.

I call this book a guide because I'm going to guide you through everything you need to know about working on TV, movie, commercial and music video sets as an extra or background actor. You will also learn how to work with known actors, get well paid and have the time of your life all while on your vacation.

The only difference between people who work on TV and movies as background actors and the people who don't, is that the people who work, signed up to be there.

Being involved in the making of a TV show or movie is just as exciting as you can imagine. Keep in mind that some of your favorite stars probably began their careers as background actors themselves.

One exciting thing about this business is that you never know who you are going to see or where you are going to be filming. Every day is different. One day you could be working at an airport, the next, in the crowd of a concert, or on the beach in Malibu. Each day spent working as a background actor is exciting and new.

Television and film are not only forms of entertainment, but art. You'll see many fascinating things you're not able to see anywhere else, or in any other industry. On set, you're going to see how every little part of the production is put together to make a magical piece of entertainment. Trust me when I tell you, you'll never look at television or movies the same way after you've worked on one.

You will see creativity in set design: the transformation of an empty room into a cafe, an old newspaper building into a police precinct, or an abandoned hospital into a breeding ground for zombies.

You are going to be up close and personal with actors, directors, costume designers, make-up and hair artists and the rest of the talented crew. You will experience the whole amazing process!

Once you've worked in this industry, you'll have stories to tell your friends and family. So, the next time you visit Los Angeles, why not be an insider looking out, rather than an outsider looking in!

If you've decided to play a part, so to speak, in this exciting world of being an extra or a background actor – welcome!

Part One: Preparation

Chapter 1: Stories of Two Tourists Who Became Background Actors

In this chapter you are going to hear the stories of how two tourists, while on vacation, not only signed up to be extras, but how one of them decided to stay in Los Angeles and is still successfully working to this day.

Both of these actors love their experiences working in the industry. And while there are no guarantees that you will be as successful as they've been, or that you will find work as easily, remember, persistence and tenacity are the names of the game when you are pursuing any job you love.

Rome's story

Originally from New York, Rome moved to Iowa, where he worked with a large transportation company for several years before moving to Los Angeles.

"I came to Los Angeles on vacation in 2005. I found out from a friend about working in the movie business as an extra. It really was as easy as just going in and signing up with the casting agency. I filled out an information form describing my character type and my skills. They took a digital photo of me and downloaded everything onto their computer database.

"The process concluded with me being supplied with the telephone number to the casting agency's work line. I called in and listened to a recorded message regarding descriptions of the types of extras they were casting.

When I heard a description of something I thought I'd be a good fit for, I called the number the casting director supplied and submitted myself. Then if the agency decides to book you, they will tell you what character you will be playing. They'll give you another phone number to call for the wardrobe description and directions to the job.

"The more persistent you are, the more work you will get. A word of advice – if the casting agency is looking for a specific type, don't call unless you fit the role. If they are looking for extras who are 30 to 40 years of age, but you are 60, don't call! If you are Asian, but they are looking for African Americans, don't call! It is a waste of their time and makes you look unprofessional.

"After my lengthy vacation, I decided to stay. The highpoint of my career thus far is having the pleasure to have been directed by an Academy Award-winning director who gave me personal instruction.

"I'm currently a regular background actor on a prime time drama and having the time of my life."

Sam's Story

Sam is a pharmacist by trade and a Florida resident. "In 1981, traveled to California on vacation. While taking a Hollywood studio tour, I was told about the world of becoming an extra and fell in love with the idea. I took the opportunity to sign-up with a casting company. Even though I went on the studio tours, I wanted to be directly involved. Ever since then, from August to March each year during the TV season, I do background work. In between I do my pharmacy work.

"I do a lot of background work. I've worked on numerous television shows and have had a blast.

"I'd say, be persistent. Don't give up. Accept rejection but don't take it personally. Be vigilant and sign-up with as many casting companies as you can. I called several times a day because roles are being cast throughout the day.

You'll find jobs are on the work line one minute, and can be gone the next. One of the most interesting roles I've had was as a nice dead body. I registered with at least four or five casting companies. It's all timing. Being in the right place at the right time. It takes a bit of dedication."

NOTES

_____

_____

_____

_____

_____

_____

_____

_____

_____

_____

_____

_____

_____

_____

Chapter 2: Signing Up!

To start working, you'll need to sign-up with casting agencies (See the Appendix for a few agencies).

Sometimes, vacationers may hesitate, thinking, "Well, I'm only in L.A. for two weeks and I may not have the time," or, "I don't think I fit into any particular type they are looking for."

Remember, the hardest part of doing something new is taking that first step. If you've ever worked for a temp agency, you will understand how relatively easy this whole process is.

Don't slip into a frame of mind thinking, "I'm not thin, pretty, or young enough." Casting agents look for actors of all shapes and sizes to play a myriad of varying roles. Maybe they'll need nondescript looking people to walk down the street behind the principal actors. They aren't looking for models to fill those roles. They are looking for real people and this probably means you.

Let me also say that you need no prior experience to work as a background actor. It is more important that you have the right look so that you can be a fit for the type of background actor the casting agency is seeking.

Once you sign-up with a casting agency, they will put you into their database. They will categorize you by the type they think you will be cast as. We will discuss types at the end of Chapter 3.

When you first call the casting agency to sign-up, find out when their non-union registration days are. Some agencies allow you to register online. With the larger agencies, you'll need to go to their office in person. Be sure to arrive 45 minutes before the sign-up time or you will be turned away. They will sign-up extras for that day. Once they reach capacity, they send everyone home.

These are the items you must bring with you to casting registration: a valid driver's license, state issued photo ID, or a passport, along with your Social Security card. THESE ITEMS ARE MUSTS! There are no exceptions.

Just before you sign-up, you'll be given a registration form, and there will be an orientation about the casting agency. They will explain how to fill out your registration form which includes your name and contact information. In addition, you'll also be asked to write in what character type you think you are. (Average looking, hipster, high school, biker, gang member, military, etc.). Your age range, and what specialty wardrobe you have. (Tuxedo, military, police, medical, etc.).

Make sure you dress in the appropriate wardrobe and wear a hairstyle that fits your type. For example, doctor, lawyer, office type, wear a suit or business attire. Musicians, rockers and biker types, wear a leather jacket, jeans and boots. If you are unsure, Google images of your category for examples of your look. If you think you can be more than one type, write that on the form as well.

Also, if you have tattoos or piercings, indicate that on the form and mention the areas of the body they are located.

You will list any special skills or abilities you have, such as swimming, fencing, or if you can ride a horse. Be honest about what you can or cannot do. If you can't ride a horse, you certainly don't want to waste the production's time and money when they find out you can't do the skill they want.

You won't need to bring photos because the agency will take a digital photo of you which will be used by the casting directors to cast from.

Your car can be also be a star, used as a picture car; one of many cars on TV shows and movies seen parked on streets, or driving by. You'll be asked to fill out the information about your car; the year, color, and model, (red, white or black cars are not useable. This can also include campers, trucks and SUVs). You'll be fully compensated if you are booked with your vehicle.

Finally, you will be provided with a casting information phone number, and Twitter and Facebook casting pages where jobs are posted throughout the day, (see Appendix).

Now you can start searching for jobs. Each casting agency posts in real time casting information, via Twitter, Facebook or casting phone lines. These posts provide details of what they are looking for, for various roles for a particular day, along with the phone number of the casting director you are to call.

Only respond to the type(s) you think you are. For example, if they are looking for men in their 30s for a bar scene, don't apply if you are a female in your 50s. If you feel you are right for that role, call the number provided by the casting director to submit yourself for that production. In some cases you will be asked to email your information which usually consists of your name and contact number.

If you don't see or hear a part that you are right for keep checking every few minutes. New jobs are posted throughout the day. (Helpful hint - if you'd like to receive alerts about new casting posts on your phone, or pad, go to Twitter and turn on the notification option. This way you'll receive an alert every time a new job is posted.

Keep in mind, like many job opportunities, this is a very competitive business. Therefore, if you hear or see a post you are right for, you need to jump on it immediately. Sure enough, someone else will grab it during the moment you were pondering whether or not you should take it. Remember, a lot of people are also looking for these jobs. You will have competition.

If you really want to be on television or have a part in a movie remember, be persistent. Don't give up. Accept rejection but don't take it personally. Be vigilant and sign-up with as many casting agencies as you can.

You are on your way!

NOTES

_____

_____

_____

_____

_____

_____

_____

_____

_____

_____

_____

_____

_____

_____

Chapter 3: Outfitting Yourself

Now you'll learn how to decide what character look you are, and learn which clothes to pack that you'll need as potential wardrobe to fit your character type.

What you look like is almost as important as the role you are going to play. In fact, they go hand in hand because what you look like denotes your character, or tells the audience what you are all about. For example, from a man's haircut you can usually tell if a person is a boy-next-door, a CEO, a football player, or a rocker. Clothing can make the audience come to their own assumptions. They will perceive you as a conservative type, or a bit rebellious depending on your outfit.

First, I will go over some of the wardrobe you will need to bring with you. Then I will discuss how to maneuver through wardrobe and makeup and what will be provided for you. I have outlined this for both men and women, including what to carry your items in and what you can bring to the holding area.

The holding area is where you and other extras stay until you are needed on the set. Remember that while you are working, security will protect the holding area. There is also security on set. So, don't worry about leaving your property in the holding area. But, always use your best judgment regarding your belongings.

Some Basic Character Types:

- Hip and trendy

- Conservative, business type

- 18 to look younger (Are you older than 18, but look younger?)

- Biker

- Homeless

- Upscale

- Rock and roller

- Hooker

- Dead Body

Casting directors will describe a character type they're looking for. You'll need to have the proper wardrobe to fit that type. I'll now go over the basic clothes you'll need to bring as your wardrobe selections. I have outlined this for both men and women, including what you'll need to carry your wardrobe items in.

Packing Basic Wardrobe and Accessories

For Men
- One dark suit (not black). Blue or gray is best.

- Two dress shirts in ivory, blue or gray.   No white, loud colors, stripes or prints!

- One pair of dark pants in blue or gray.

- One pair of jeans that can be worn with the suit jacket.

- One pair of conservative shorts.

- Three interchangeable ties.

- Two sweaters in muted colors such as green, brown, blue or burgundy.

- One pair of khaki colored pants.

- Two different polo style shirts.

- One winter coat.

- Thermal underwear in case you work at night, in cold weather, or on a cold set.

- Three pairs of black socks.

- One pair of black soft-soled shoes.

- One pair of tennis shoes with white socks.

- Pack a small umbrella (just in case.)

- One scarf, a pair of gloves, and a hat to match in case you are in a winter scene.

For Women
- One dark suit with a skirt (no black). Blue or gray is best.

- Two blouses in ivory, blue or gray. No white, loud colors, stripes or prints!

- One pair of dark pants (that match the suit).

- One pair of jeans that can be worn with the

suit jacket.

- One pair of conservative shorts.

- Two sweaters in muted colors such as green, brown, blue or burgundy.

- One winter coat.

- Thermal underwear in case you work at night, in cold weather, or on a cold set.

- One pair soft-soled shoes either with low heels or flats.

- One pair of panty hose that match your skin tone.

- One pair of tennis shoes with white socks.

- Pack a small umbrella (just in case.)

- One or two scarves, gloves, and a hat to match in case you are in a winter scene.

Make sure your jewelry matches what you are wearing. If in doubt, go as conservative as possible. Put your jewelry in a lock-tight plastic bag so that the wardrobe department can decide if they want you to wear it or not. Arrive on the set without wearing earrings, watches, necklaces or any personal jewelry.

Do not use any cologne, perfume, or aftershave. Too many fragrances in a small, enclosed area can be sickening. Some individuals are even allergic. Be considerate.

Wear normal makeup and style your hair naturally. You will be touched up throughout the day on set, if needed. Don't wear or bring any loud colors – no bright red or orange. Nail polish should be clear, or soft colored. French tips are okay.

Some General Tips

Bring your clothing in a garment or wardrobe bag. Some people prefer a suitcase with wheels because it is easier not to carry a bag. Keep a jacket or sweater handy. The temperature can easily be in the upper 90's outside and very chilly inside of a studio. Think layers.

For foot comfort here is a great tip: Use cushioned inner soles in all your shoes for extra comfort. You will thank me later. In addition, bring a portable shoe shine pad. The wardrobe department will want your shoes to be clean and shiny. These are available in the shoe section of most drug stores.

Whatever else you need will be supplied by the wardrobe department. If production wants to switch out your pants for another type of garment, they will supply that, as well.

Make sure there are NO designer or other labels visible on the clothing or you can't wear them. This means no logos of any type.

One fun tidbit about clothing from the wardrobe department, you never know who previously wore what they give you. Look at the label. Some studios have wardrobe has been around since the 1930s. You might wear a gown from the golden age of Hollywood or the same jacket a blockbuster star wore!

NOTES

_____

_____

_____

_____

_____

_____

_____

_____

_____

_____

_____

_____

_____

_____

Chapter 4: Understanding Your Role

Keep in mind that all actors are also background actors. On set, you'll see the stars of a show in scenes where they're in the background adding realism, atmosphere, and detail. Principal actors are the ones with spoken lines (dialogue), but principal actors may also do background work in certain scenes. Think of the background actors you've seen in various movies and TV shows. They are so professional you barely notice them. Your attention was on the principal speaking actors. If a background actor does his job properly, he blends perfectly into the scene.

So, you've decided you want to be a background actor and you've outfitted yourself with the necessary wardrobe. Now you need to get into the right frame of mind and prepare yourself to understand your role.

Movies and TV shows are a collaborative effort. A huge group of people work long hours to create the magic that we all see on the screen. Background actors are crucial because they add realism to the scene.

Remember, as part of the background, you are responsible for the atmosphere, the realism, and the authenticity of the scene. Think of the enormity of large- scale movies, action films, westerns, science fiction, period, or disaster films. They would not have been expressed as believably and poignantly without the hundreds of background actors in the film.

The information I'm sharing will help prepare you for your day of work on set so that you come across as a professional. Being prepared is as important as being on time. So, how do you prepare?

Keep in mind five key things:
1. Listen carefully.
2. Follow directions.
3. Make your actions look natural.
4. Mime only! Don't talk or speak your reactions.
5. Walk softly, literally.

I can't stress these five key things enough!

To prepare for your role, the night before, try to watch a similar type of program, whether it's a sitcom or drama, to familiarize yourself with the type of background actions you may be asked to perform. (You never thought you'd ever have a job that required watching TV was part of your homework and preparation, did you?)

Remember, you are a significant part of the entire television and movie making process. Where else can you work with a possible Emmy© or Oscar© winning director, wardrobe designer, makeup artist or production designer?

Later, when you're back home and telling your friends and neighbors all about your experiences on set, you'll be able to say, "I was a part of that!"

NOTES

_____

_____

_____

_____

_____

_____

_____

_____

_____

_____

_____

_____

_____

_____

Chapter 5: Readiness

You want to hit the ground running your first day as a background actor. You want to be ready. What does this mean? It means find a hotel or motel located centrally to the studios. Most of the work for background actors is in Los Angeles, Hollywood, Burbank and Culver City. You don't want to be located on the fringe of this vast city or you'll have a long and time consuming commute. You might want to go online and take a look at a map of the particular areas you'll be working in.

Being ready means you're on time, dressed, hair and makeup done, with wardrobe and voucher in hand. Being ready means you're set to begin work.

Before you arrive at the studio or location, prepare in advance as much as possible. Fill up your gas tank, have your street or freeway directions ready, lay out the necessary clothing, pack your garment bag and don't forget to set your alarm!! The last thing you need to worry about is waiting in line at a gas station and risk being late.

Be aware, you are responsible for your own transportation to the studio or location. Make sure you leave with plenty of time to get to your destination. Preparation is essential because you must be on time.

In most cities, public transportation can get you anywhere you need to go. In Los Angeles, everything is spread out, and the location may not be easy to get to. A car is highly recommended. You have several options - rent a car, drive your own, Uber or taxi cab.

The night before you are scheduled to work, you will have received your call time, wardrobe instructions, and your location from casting either via text, or a direct phone call. How you get specific directions to the location is up to you. Most people use a phone or a laptop to get directions on the Internet. You can choose to purchase a map or you can simply use GPS.

Don't be intimidated getting around Los Angeles or any of the smaller cities where TV shows and movies are made, or getting on studio lots. If you're not used to big city driving and don't want to navigate the freeways, you can call the auto club (if you're a member) or check with your hotel desk staff or concierge service. They can help you work out a route using surface streets.

In the world of TV and movies, time is money. Give yourself plenty of time to find and arrive at your destination, taking into consideration any traffic, road or even location changes, and/or obstacles that might cause a delay.

Be dressed properly. Arrive dressed in your character's clothing, with any specific changes in your garment bag. Make sure all of your clothes are clean, pressed and ready to wear. Your shoes need to be cleaned and shined. Unless of course, you're portraying a homeless person or scruffy shoes were specified.

For women only: Your hair is styled and make-up is on; nothing elaborate, just your regular hair style and makeup. Please, no curlers or wet hair, unless that's the specific look you were asked for.

Everyone must bring their garment bag with them, together with, your backpack or purse. Don't forget your photo ID, studio lot pass, and have your voucher in hand. This is readiness. You're good to go. You're ready to work.

NOTES

_____

_____

_____

_____

_____

_____

_____

_____

_____

_____

_____

_____

_____

Chapter 6: IDs, Vouchers and Payment

You will soon experience the excitement and thrill of being an extra. Since it is a job, you can also experience the excitement and thrill of getting paid!

Keep in mind that if you do begin working as a background actor, you'll be considered a non-union extra which means you don't belong to the union known as SAG-AFTRA (Screen Actors Guild-American Federation of Television and Radio Artists).

Let's now address the identification (ID) you are required to have on you at all times while on the set, how to fill out and understand your voucher, and a bit about payment for your services.

ID (Identification)

Security is necessary on studio lots and sets. Just like many other places of employment such as banks, you are to either wear a name tag or have your ID on you. In the film industry, you must have ID just to get onto the studio lot. This can be your state issued driver's license or ID card, your passport, and your Social Security card. You'll be required to have your photo ID on you at all times.

If you happen to leave the lot at any time, you must have your photo ID and your studio pass with you in order to re-enter the lot. You might also have to go through the same entrance procedures as you did when you first arrived.

What do you do once you arrive on the studio lot? It will almost be like checking in at the airport.

If you're driving to the studio, you'll be directed where to enter the lot and where to park. For location shoots, you'll be directed to the crew parking. If you are not parking on the lot, or you are taking public transportation, or being dropped off, simply go to the studio entrance you were directed to report to.

You'll go to the studio security booth. They will look for your name on their list provided by the casting agency and check your photo ID. They might ask you what show you're working on. Be prepared to have your purse, garment bag, and other belongings searched. You might have to pass through a metal detector. You will then be issued a studio pass. This will get you on the lot. Your ID will be handed back to you and you'll be directed where to go to start work.

If for some reason your name's not on security's production list, don't panic. This does happen occasionally for whatever reason. Ask the security guard to call the production office or casting agency to straighten things out. If you're unsure of anything, ask questions. The security guards are very helpful.

It's very important that you keep your studio lot pass with you at all times. Studios take security very seriously and so should you.

A studio audience might arrive for a sitcom you are working on. If you're outside the holding area or off the set without your studio pass and photo ID, how does security know you didn't just sneak on the lot with that audience? Make it easy for security to do their job. They need to know you are a working background actor on a production for that day.

VOUCHERS

A voucher is another name for a time card. If you've worked for a large company, you may be familiar with this process. The voucher is sent from the casting agency to the job and will be there waiting for you.

Vouchers from casting agencies can vary in appearance and will provide payroll with all the necessary information to issue your paycheck. A voucher usually has your name pre-printed on it and will show your call time, the date you work, the name of the production company, and the title of the show you will work on. There will also be an area on the voucher for the lunch period and your set dismissal time.

When you arrive at the sound stage, location, or the base camp (which could be very early in the morning), you will be greeted by someone from the crew or a production assistant (PA) who handles the background or extras. You'll check in with them and they will give you your voucher. The voucher should also show the pay rate you'll earn for the day. Fill in your name (if needed), the address where you want your check mailed, and any other necessary information.

Make sure all the information on your voucher is correct. Write in your Social Security number and sign it. There will be someone on set who can show you how to fill it out correctly. Be sure to let them know this is your first time filling it out. Don't be afraid to ask for any type of help.

You'll quickly get used to filling out vouchers. Vouchers are assigned for each day you work. This can be viewed as either a bit time consuming or really great because you'll be mailed a check for each day you work.

These vouchers can also be held hostage, so to speak, because you will be required to turn them over to the wardrobe or property department in exchange for the costume or prop you'll need for that day.

At the end of the day, you will return the costume or prop, get your voucher back, and finish filling it out. You will fill in your payroll information (W-2 or I-9 information) which includes the number of deductions you'll want for income tax purposes. When you are finished, the PA will tear off the back sheet of your voucher and hand it to you for your records.

PAYMENT

One great thing about working for the studios is being well compensated for your time. They will pay you for eight hours work whether you work one minute, or all eight hours. If you show up for a job and they decide they don't need you for that day, you will be paid for eight hours work. Overtime for non-union workers is time and a half.

After ten hours you will be paid a rate of double time.

Upgrades – Sometimes you may be asked to do something which will upgrade you to a union rate; in either a background or principal part. On a rare occasion you may be upgraded to a principal status by the director and asked to speak. Again, this rarely happens, but when it does, it will turn out to be a wonderful experience and payday.

NOTES

_____

_____

_____

_____

_____

_____

_____

_____

_____

_____

_____

_____

_____

_____

Part Two: Now You're All Set

Chapter7: Your First Day on Set

You have booked your first job and you're ready for your first day on the set. You have your photo I.D. with you and your wardrobe, which is clean, pressed and packed in your garment bag. You've parked your car, have received your studio pass and found your way on the lot or location where you are filming for that day.

As mentioned in Chapter 6, you will proceed to the base camp which is a gathering area for production. (If you have trouble finding it, make sure to ask security when you enter the studio lot or location on how to get there). Once there, you will get further instructions for the day by an AD or PA. They will also provide you with your voucher.

After you fill in the voucher, you'll typically head over to catering for breakfast, where you can pretty much order anything you like. Be polite and considerate of others when you wait in line. Craft Services (often referred to as crafty), is a designated area that provides snack food and is a courtesy for everyone. However, don't cram six or seven granola bars into your backpack. Craft Services is not a free store. Get what you need and go back to the holding area to eat. Be extremely careful not to spill food on your wardrobe!

Wardrobe

After breakfast you'll be directed to wardrobe. They will look at the outfit you've been instructed to bring for that day. If the wardrobe department doesn't like the items you've brought, they will issue you alternative wardrobe and take your voucher.

Hair and Makeup

After your wardrobe has been approved, you may be taken over to hair and makeup to be given the okay from those departments.

Props

    If production decides to issue you a prop, you need to take your voucher (time card) with you to the prop department. They will hold your voucher until the end of the day in exchange for when you return the prop.

    Remember, you are responsible for your prop. Make sure you keep track of everything you're given. Have your prop ready to go when you are called on set. If you lose or misplace your prop, immediately report it to an assistant director (AD), so they can help you locate or replace it. If you are carrying a heavy prop ask someone in charge if there is a safe place you can put it until you are called to the set.

If the PA doesn't send you to hair and make- up or props, you'll go to the holding area.

Holding Area

The holding area is the background actor's trailer or a room, so to speak. It's your resting area, with chairs for everyone. Just claim a chair, place your property (garment bag, etc.) on it, and you're set. You might be provided a rack to hang your clothes on. If not, you'll need to find a spot to neatly store your belongings.

Now you sit and wait until you are called to the set. It's always best to keep your property stored away so that you can to be ready to go onto the set at a moment's notice. Obviously, you don't want to leave your wallet open on your chair while you're on set so remember to use your best judgment with your belongings.

Never, ever, remove someone else's property from a chair to take it as your own. If there aren't enough chairs in the holding area, simply bring this to the attention of the PA. The movie and TV business can be summed up by the expression,

"Hurry up and wait." There's a lot of down time in a background actor's life. When in the holding area, with careful planning, there are a few things you can bring that will make your job a lot easier and help time pass more quickly. Keep yourself entertained while waiting and stay alert.

When you are in holding, you can use this time to be on your laptop, tablet, or phone (don't forget your charger). Do social media, read a book or use an e-reader, play cards, socialize with other extras, make phone calls and especially network. Bring a DVD player with earbuds, or a sketch pad and pencils. Many people play video games or knit, crochet or do needlepoint.

You must stay focused and alert. You can nap in the holding area if you really need to, but a better idea is to bring items that will help you pass the time. Always clean up after yourself. Be conscious of your litter (candy wrappers, coffee cups, etc.).

If the holding area is too warm or too cold, let the PA or AD know. Don't hesitate to bring necessary information to their attention. If you need to leave the holding area and go to the restroom, or have a smoke, always let a PA or AD know. The term used is "10/1" as in, "I'm taking a 10/1."

There will be designated areas for smokers outside of the holding area. Obviously, no drugs or alcohol ever! If you bring these with you, you'll be asked to leave.

Professionals on the set don't want extras hanging around asking questions while they work. Again, time is money. Part of your job is to stay in the holding area and entertain yourself until you're asked to come on set and provide the scene's background action.

Anything that you leave in holding must be put away when you are called to the set. Even though the holding area has security, you don't want to leave your property out in the open.

There are two exceptions to be aware of:

1. If you're working on a location away from the studio lot, then the holding area for the background actors will most likely be chairs set up under a tent. Alternatively, chairs may be set up against a wall or in a room at a specific location. There's always a security guard stationed in the holding area on a location shoot. Once again, if your possessions are zipped up in your bags and on your chair, you should be okay. If you feel uncomfortable, inform the PA or AD that you want to keep your purse or bag with you.

2. A "large call" is defined as 50 to over 100 background actors or more. Obviously, the more people on a set, the more hectic it will be. It will also be harder for security to know who should or should not be there. A smart thing to do is to drape your jacket or garment bag over all of

your property. Make sure any valuables you bring to the set, or on location, fit in your bag. You're already aware of the basic clothing a background actor needs to have (see Chapter 2).

One of the most fun aspects of being a background actor is that you're going to meet so many incredibly creative people in holding. You may find you don't have to reach for that novel or video game after all. There's a lot of waiting involved, but if you prepare in advance, you can keep busy.

NOTES

_____

_____

_____

_____

_____

_____

_____

_____

_____

_____

_____

_____

_____

_____

Chapter 8: Rules and Etiquette on the Set

Good etiquette on set is essential. You're working in an enclosed space with many people for long hours. Here are a few rules you need to know to begin working like a professional on the set:

- Listen for instruction.
- Don't talk to the principal actors and never, ever ask for an autograph.
- When on set, do your work.
- Never eat or drink on set, unless directed to.
- Keep all food in the craft services area or holding area.
- Pay attention to everything that is going on, on the set.
- Remember the directions you are given and remember where you were. You're going to have to remember and repeat specific actions several times, so pay close attention and ask questions.

- If anything is unclear. If you receive contradictory directions, don't be afraid to ask for clarification

- Don't enter a studio when a red light is flashing.

- Never talk while cameras are rolling, mime only.

- There are no electronics allowed on set. This means no cell phones, tablets, cameras, pagers, etc. These are all left in the holding area.

- Be aware of equipment that will be crossing through from time to time: cameras, cables, crew, and who's moving where. Stay sharp.

- Walk softly while on set. Don't make noise.

- If you are too sick to report to work, call the casting agency and let them know so they can replace you.

- If you become injured or ill at work, let someone from production know immediately.

- Fresh breath and a clean body are an essential courtesy to others. Use gum or breath mints (available at Craft Services), but get rid of it before you go on set.

- When meals are served, cast and crew are always fed first. They have to get right back to work after eating, while background actors will probably return to the holding area until instructed to return to set.

If there's anything you're not sure of, ask questions.

Experienced people on the set are usually generous with newcomers. They want to help you do your best.

It's important to be enthusiastic, look like you are having a good time and enjoying what you are doing.

If you follow these simple suggestions, you'll have a productive day on the job and soon find yourself with a reputation as a professional.

NOTES

76

Chapter 9: Catering and Craft Services

What can you expect when it comes to food? You'll get one of two things – catering or Craft Services.

Catering

On a typical morning, food will be set up in the catering area. Breakfast may include foods like eggs, pancakes, hash browns, bacon, French toast, a breakfast burrito, omelets (which usually includes an omelet bar), hot and cold cereal, bagels, bread (toasters available), doughnuts and muffins. Condiments are readily available. There may be a fruit tray, assorted juices, milk, coffee and tea - everything necessary for your morning caffeine fix.

Lunch/dinner may include a variety of meats, vegetable dishes, potato salad, macaroni salad, green salads, or a pasta bar. One day there may be Mexican food or Thai food. There may be trays of tomato slices with herbs, marinated mushrooms or artichokes, grape leaves, calamari, and more.

There may be various breads and a variety of delicious desserts. Cheesecake, pie, yogurt, brownie cake, ice cream and even warm cookies.

When lunch and dinner are catered everyone will have a place to sit and eat. You'll have either a half hour or hour for lunch, and as said before, cast and crew will go first because they have to get back to work immediately. A cool thing about a catered lunch, or dinner, is that you never know who you might sit next to. Many times actors and directors sit with the crew.

Craft Services (Crafty)

During the course of the day, craft services usually provides a variety of snacks like muffins, donuts, chips, candy, and cookies along with coffee and tea and some fruit are available. Other foods that may be included are sandwiches, salads, pizza, soups, chili and Chinese food.

There are usually four or five big ice chests that are filled with bottled water, milk, diet and regular soda, juices and sports drinks. Coffee and tea are always available.

Crafty is a grab and go set up, so, select your food, and head back to the holding area. Later in the day, after lunch/dinner, crafty usually serves a second meal, which can range from pizza to Chinese food and salads to sandwiches.

If you have food restrictions, for dietary or religious reasons, consider bringing your own meals.

NOTES

_____

_____

_____

_____

_____

_____

_____

_____

_____

_____

_____

_____

_____

Part Three: What's Next?

Chapter 10: Going to the TV or Movie Set

In most cases, an AD will come to holding and give a brief breakdown of shots expected to be accomplished that day. They'll give you an approximate warning time for when you'll be taken to the set. This will usually be announced as, "This is your ten-minute warning." During this time you should use the restroom, straighten your outfit, fix your hair, and be picture perfect and ready to work. You should be prepared to respond right away when called to set.

On your way to set, production may decide to issue you a prop. Props can range from a book, newspaper, a briefcase, etc. You may be asked to bring your voucher to the prop department. If so, be prepared to hand over your voucher in exchange for the prop(s). They will hold your voucher until the end of the day. Then you'll get it back when you return the prop(s). Remember, you are responsible for your prop. Keep track of every item you are given. If you lose or misplace your prop, immediately report it to the AD, so they can help you locate or replace it. Next, the AD will guide you to set and position you for the scene.

Once placed, you'll be given instructions as to your particular action for the scene. For instance the AD may ask you to walk across the set, (walk naturally, don't walk like a zombie or robot unless you've been instructed to do so) or, you might be directed to talk to a "friend" (miming, of course!), or to pick up a book, giving the appearance that activity or action is going on behind the principal actors while they are executing their parts.

Extras might pretend to dine in restaurants, react at sporting events, hang out in bars, work in offices, stand in lines, and interact with other background actors (miming). Try to behave as naturally and realistically as possible. For example, if you're in a bar scene, think about what you'd normally do. You might chat, greet someone, be cheerful, laugh, answer a phone or order a drink. Remember, the AD will give you all the necessary directions.

You'll do a few rehearsals before the scene is shot. The AD will then yell, "Final touches!" This involves the hair, makeup, and wardrobe departments rechecking both principal actors and extras before the camera rolls.

When you hear the AD say, "Picture's up!" it means they are ready to shoot a scene. (Study the Glossary in the back of this book and become familiar with any on set lingo that may be used.)

When the crew is ready to begin filming, you'll hear, "Rolling!" This will be followed by an assistant camera person who steps in front of the camera with a slate or clapper. He will give the name of the production and the take number, snap the clapper and step away. Then you will hear the camera department yell, "Set." Then, when ready, the director will yell, "and ... action." This is when you will execute the direction you've been given for the scene.

At the conclusion of the scene the AD will yell, "Cut, reset!" That means they want you to go back to your starting position. Pay strict attention to what is going on and where you were in the scene.

Sometimes the scene will be shot from multiple angles. Keep in mind that they can only shoot in one direction at a time because the crew can only be on one side. You might be moved to the other side and shot from the opposite direction, if they so desire. They will call out, "Turning!" or "Coming around!"

When they finish up the sequence you'll hear, "Checking the gate!" It means this portion of the scene is done.

Most scenes are anywhere from two to eight pages. This can take around eight hours to shoot. Dramas take longer to shoot because only one or two cameras are used and require numerous set-ups. If you work on a sitcom, four cameras are usually used. And, it might be shot in front of a live studio audience.

During this time, keep in mind what was discussed regarding the rules for behavior on set. It may be tempting to ask for an autograph from one of the principals or take a photograph of them. Rein in any desire to do so. You may be asked to leave the set and have your camera confiscated by production.

Usually, after six hours of work you will break for lunch. The AD or PA will announce when lunch is, whether it is catered or a walk-away, whether it is a half hour or one hour, and what time you'll need to be back in holding and ready for work.

After lunch, you might be checked by hair, make- up, and wardrobe again and then continue to shoot until the end of the day. Your work day will depend on how many scenes you are in.

It's crucial that, once you're on set, you pay attention to everything. Be aware of what's around you. Be careful of walls, set dressings, any props, etc. The crew is constantly making adjustments. They'll come through with lights and equipment. Be aware of what people say. Listen!

You'll hear crew members say things like:
• "Watch your back" (Someone's coming up behind you with equipment).
• "Watch your eyes" (Strong lights are added or turned on).
• "Flashing" (Someone's coming through with a camera to take a photo of the set, hair, costumes or makeup for continuity. The photo is needed to recreate the scene perfectly.)

Some shout outs are obvious:
- "Watch the cord."
- "Clear the set."
- "Step away for a minute."
- "Background, back to holding."
- "You can go relax" (Go back to holding).

A hot set is a set that has already been filmed. It's crucial, for the sake of continuity, that everything remains exactly the same from scene to scene.

Continuity issues to remember include: listen carefully to the AD: "This is the scene. Here's what you're going to do and what your action will be."

- The AD will give you your crosses (moving across the set) or your action, which could be simply moving a file in an office, picking up a phone, or walking across a room.
- The AD will tell you when this action must be done There are two types of cues or signals for a background actor to make their move – an action cue or a line cue. I'm going to give you an example of each.
- The AD will explain your cue, for example:

"Two actors walk into the room and sit down during the scene.

Your action cue is when they sit down, you will cross the room." Every time they shoot the scene from a different camera angle, be prepared to do that same cross at the same time of that action cue.

The AD could give you a verbal cue, for example: "Once both actors sit down in the scene and you hear one of them say, 'I have to make a phone call.' That is your cue to cross the room."

A helpful hint: Ask the AD what the dialogue is just before your line cue. It's easy to blink or cough and completely miss your cue. Until you're proficient at picking up line cues, it's smart to know a line or two of dialogue just before your cue. It really helps.

When, "Background action!" is called, that's your signal to watch for your action cue or listen for your verbal cue.

You may be asked to start and stop action at any point within that scene. The AD might say, "We're going to pick it up just before the guys sit down in their chairs." Remember to do your cross at the directed action or line cue.

There are people on set to help with continuity. The PA, the AD and the Script Supervisor will all help you; they'll remind you of where you were. Listen carefully.

Every article of clothing must be fixed. Your shirt needs to be tucked in or un-tucked depending on how it was before. Your collar and tie has to be the same. If it was straight when you began, you have to check and make sure it's still straight (unless you're instructed otherwise).

Don't mess around with your wardrobe once it's in place. Don't take off your jacket or roll up your sleeves if they've already shot the scene with your jacket on.

After each take, fix yourself so you look exactly the same. Make sure your hair is smooth. Look down and make sure nothing's hiked up or really out of place.

If you work multiple days, remember, continuity is crucial. You must wear the same wardrobe, and the same hairstyle. Women:

Don't change your lipstick or eye-shadow colors. They must remain the same. Men: If you had a mustache, don't shave it off!

At the end of the day you'll know you are almost finished because you'll hear, "Abby Singer!" It means this is the second to last shot of the day.

When you hear, "Martini shot!" that means it's the last shot of the day. Then it's, "Checking the gate!" Finally you'll hear, "That's a wrap!" You are finished shooting for the day.

NOTES

_____

_____

_____

_____

_____

_____

_____

_____

_____

_____

_____

_____

_____

Chapter 11: Wrap and Signing Out

Next is check out time: If you've been issued a prop, you'll return it to the property department. If you've been issued any wardrobe you'll return any pieces that were given to you to the wardrobe department. Remember to get your voucher back from either department. Then you'll go to the PA who will sign your time card and release you for the day. Make sure that your voucher is signed and completely filled out and that you've received your copy for your records.

Before you leave, you might be told if they need you the next day, or if you are done on that job.

You've now completed your first day on a set. Congratulations!

NOTES

_____

_____

_____

_____

_____

_____

_____

_____

_____

_____

_____

_____

_____

Chapter 12: Booking Your Next Job

You're in Los Angeles for a vacation, or perhaps you live here. You've signed up with a casting agency, and maybe you've already experienced your first day on a set as a background actor. You loved your experience on set and want to do more. So, how do you get your next gig?

First of all, common sense rules of proper behavior and etiquette as discussed are "no-brainer" suggestions for increasing the chances that you'll be called for more work.

In addition to your professional focus, add persistence and networking to the list of skills to hone so you keep getting the gigs.

Persistence
As with any job you really want, you have to go after it. This is especially true in the acting business. You have to be persistent calling

in for jobs. There are dozens of people in line for the job you want. Sometimes the call line is busy, or the job you want is already off the call line. Don't give up! Maintain your persistence, and keep calling to see what else is available (See Chapter 2 regarding calling casting agencies).

Network

Engage your networking skills so you can keep getting background acting jobs. Since you've spent some time in holding you've probably seen other actors checking Twitter or Facebook on their phones to find what jobs are available for the next day. You should be doing the same thing.

Everyone in holding is networking and looking for their next job. This is just a part of the daily routine. If you aren't sure who to call, or what jobs are available, ask. People will share information with you. One thing about actors, usually, there is great camaraderie. They have all been where you are at some time.

Getting your next gig is easier than you think. You just have to keep checking the Twitter and Facebook posts for the latest casting information. Remember don't hesitate, and make the call to get the next job.

If they call you, they will expect you to return their call within the hour. Be reachable. The best of luck!

NOTES

Chapter 13: Enjoy Yourself, You Are on Vacation After All

You've signed up, dressed up, and had the time of your life. You've gotten on studio lots. You've watched actors you admire bring their characters to life. You've worked with extremely talented, professional people on sets that sometimes seem more real than real life.

It's all incredibly exciting. But don't ever let being a working background actor prevent you from enjoying the other part of your life – your actual vacation.

You came out to Los Angeles with a definite plan to work and have fun. Make sure you balance all that time working with a little rest and relaxation.

Go to the beach! Drive up the coast. Watch a sunset over the Pacific. Spend a day or two at an amusement park. Enjoy our famous California cuisine. Sleep in. Go to one of our many museums. Have a drink by your hotel pool.

Live life to the fullest while you are in Los Angeles. It's been said we most regret the things we don't do. I personally think that's true. It's my sincere hope that the information in this book has helped you achieve your goal of working with the stars.

You've done it! You signed up for this wild and crazy, fantastic ride! Congratulations! Now get out there and enjoy the rest of your vacation!

NOTES

_____

_____

_____

_____

_____

_____

_____

_____

_____

_____

_____

_____

_____

A Summary: I've Come to L.A....Now What?

Congratulations! You've bought this book, studied it, and are well on your way to working on a television or movie set with professional actors. Whether you are here in Los Angeles permanently, or on vacation, there is nothing quite as thrilling as working on a TV or movie set and being involved in the magic of watching a show or movie getting made.

In this business, the main things to keep in mind are to be on time, be professional, and have fun!

Although working as an extra takes some time and effort, it is relatively easy to break into. There is a huge payoff. You will be working on an actual set and get to witness and enjoy an experience that you will never forget. After being involved in the TV or movie making process, you will have official bragging rights.

I hope you will find that the whole process of being on a television show or in a movie is easier than you think. Remember, the only difference between tourists who work as extras and those who do not, is that the tourists who work signed up to be there. I know you'll love your television and movie making experience!

That's a wrap!

NOTES

Glossary: On Set Lingo

Here is some on-set lingo/terminology you will find useful from your arrival until the final wrap. Everyone you'll be working with will be familiar with these terms.

10/1 – informing an AD or PA you are going to the restroom.

18 to Look Younger – you are older than 18 but can play roles that are younger than 18 so you don't have to be accompanied by a parent. For example, extras who play high school students.

1st Team – the principal actors.

2nd Team – the stand-in actors.

Abby/Abby Singer – the second to last shot of the day.

...And ...Action – when the scene REALLY starts for the principals. Rehearsal of a shot or cameras might be rolling.

Assistant Director (AD) – assists the director in any way possible to make sure he gets what he needs so the shots run smoothly.

Background Action – time to make your move.

Background Actors or Extras – people in the background.

Background Back to Holding – leave the set and go back to the holding area.

Backing it Up – you are going back a few steps from where you previously ended. You will be directed how far to back up.

Base Camp – usually on location, the main staging area where all the trailers are.

Blocking – where the actors and extras move during a scene.

Bogey – warning that a person or object is passing through called "breaching the shot."

Boom – a very long stick with a microphone at the end that is held above the actors by a sound man.

Bump – a bump is a financial increase in salary for bringing your own wardrobe, props, car, or doing something special on set that you've been asked to. The amount is negotiable.

Camera Set – the camera is ready to begin action.

Checking the Gate – means this scene is done. Usually shouted out by the 1st AD. They are checking the lensgate to visually make sure there is no hair or other objects on it. If all is good they will say, "The Gate is Good!"

Clear – get out of the way!

Coming Around/Turning Around – the camera is flipped around and the previous scene is shot from the opposite direction (This set up can take up to an hour).

Continuity – each shot, or set up, is shot at various angles. You have to repeat the exact same thing that you just did.

Copy That – this is how everyone says, "Yes," acknowledges you, or that they understand. Similar to police lingo.

Coverage – single shots of each actor during a dialogue.

Crosses – when you are walking across the set during filming.

Crossing – a courtesy warning stating that someone will be crossing in front of the camera, usually during the set-up.

Cut/Freeze – hold your position where you are until directed.

Cut/Reset – go back to your starting position. Eye-Line – the eye-line is where an actor is looking. Note: You should always avoid the actor's eye-line. It is distracting.

Final Touches – the hair, makeup, and wardrobe departments rechecking both principal actors and extras before the camera rolls.

First Assistant Director (1st AD) – is the right hand man of the director, shouts out commands (ie "picture's up" and "rolling," and runs the set and the crew.

Flashing – a courtesy verbal warning that someone is taking a reference photo.

From the Top – go back to the very beginning.

General Crew Call – the beginning of the shoot day or arrival time.

Hot Point – watch the pointy light C stand (a pipe, light stand etc.) in other words, get out of the way!

Hot Set – don't touch or move anything on the set. Everything has already been filmed or will soon resume filming. This is for continuity.

Kill That/Lose That, or make it stop now! - remove an object or turn off an obstructing light or noisy item that is disrupting the shoot.

Line Cue/Action Cue – a point in the dialogue when you make your cross or action move.

Location – a designated area where the scene will be shot (Public street, parking lot, stadium, etc.).

Lock it Up – the 1st AD will call this out when all activity and noise is to be halted because shooting is about to begin.

M.O.S. – Mit Out Sound or without sound. The scene does not require any sound to be recorded.

Make a Hole – get out of the way.

Marker – the assistant cameraman puts a slate in front of the camera and claps it for the sound department.

Martini Sequence – the last few shots of the day.

Martini Shot – the last shot of the day.

Mime – simulated speaking or simulated eating of food.

Moving On – new shot or new scene.

New Deal – they are going to do something else within the scene with additional persons.

On The Day – something you are going to do on set the day of the shoot or when they roll.

Out Time – the time you were signed out.

Picture's Up – they are ready to shoot a scene.

Production Assistant (PA) - handles the background or extras.

Pushing In/Going Tighter – a close up shot of an actor with the same action that just took place.

Rehearsal – rehearse the scene before it is shot.

Rehearsal With Background – background executes what they've been directed to do.

Rehearsal With Marks – putting marks of tape, sometimes of different colors, on the floor or ground for camera, actors, and extras positioning and lighting purposes.

Roll Camera – usually called out by the 1st AD to start the camera rolling.

Second Assistant Director (2nd AD) – in charge of background and will give you on set direction.

Soft Shoes – walk softly without looking like you are doing so.

Speed – the sound department will call this out when the sound equipment is ready to record.

Take Five – a short break usually five to ten minutes.

That's a Wrap – the last scene has been shot. You are finished shooting for the day.

Turn Around - a scene shot from the opposite direction.

Walk Away – getting lunch off set.

Walkie – refers to a walkie-talkie, which the production staff and crew use to communicate with each other on and off set.

Watch Your Back – get out of the way! Someone is coming through with equipment or an object that could hit you.

Watch Your Eyes/Striking – guard your eyes because the lighting department will be turning on a strong light.

We're on the Wrong Set – that scene is finished.

What is Your 20? – where your exact location is. Short for 10/20.

NOTES

_____

_____

_____

_____

_____

_____

_____

_____

_____

_____

_____

_____

_____

Acknowledgments

When one has been in the acting business as long as I have, there are a lot of people to thank. First and foremost, I want to thank my family for their support. Secondly, I'd like to express my gratitude to the actors I work with on a day-to-day basis for their friendship and encouragement. It has been a joy to spend countless hours working with all of you.

I couldn't have completed this book without the help of my two writers, Kimberly Kimmel and Elda Minger, and my editor, Mary B. Davis. I'd also like to thank my artist, Arne Starr for the book cover and interior sketches. Thank you all for keeping me on track, asking endless questions and organizing my years of experience as a background actor into a coherent book. I couldn't have done it without you.

And finally, this book is for all the star-struck people in the world who are highly interested in knowing more about what we as background actors do, and how to be a part of the movie making process. Next time you see an inspiring movie, or a great TV show, maybe you'll be able to say, "I was a part of that."

Appendix:

The Studios or Locations Where You Will Be Working

Los Angeles is vast, but when it gets down to it, the studios are fairly easy to get to and within a relatively close proximity to each other.

The main studios you'll find yourself working at are:

Warner Bros
4000 Warner Blvd
Burbank, CA 91505

Sony Pictures Studios
10202 W Washington Blvd
Culver City, CA 90232

Culver Studios
9336 W Washington Blvd
Culver City, CA 90232

Manhattan Beach Studios
1600 Rosecrans Avenue
Manhattan Beach, CA 90266

20 Century Fox
10201 W Pico Blvd
Los Angeles, CA 90064

Paramount Studios
5300 Melrose Ave
Hollywood, CA 90038

Raleigh Studios
5300 Melrose Ave
Hollywood, CA 90038

CBS Gower
1438 N. Gower Street
Hollywood, CA 90028

Disney Studios
500 S Buena Vista St
Burbank, CA 91505

Universal Studios
100 Universal City Plaza
Universal City, CA 91608

Santa Clarita Studios

25135 Anza Drive

Santa Clarita, CA 91355

L.A. Center Studios

1201 W 5th St T-110

Los Angeles, CA 90017

Casting Agencies

Central Casting
220 S Flower St Burbank, CA 91502
(818) 562-2755

Cut Above Casting Services
2047 N Beachwood Dr Los Angeles, CA 90068
(323) 465-3055

Jeff Olan Casting Inc.
14044 Ventura Blvd
Sherman Oaks, CA 91423 (818) 285-5462

Sande Alessi Casting
www.sandealessicasting.com

Casting Opportunities Updates

Central Casting Links

https://www.facebook.com/centralcasting/

https://twitter.com/CentralCasting

NOTES

Thank you for reading this book.

Please tell your friends about it, and leave us a comment on our Facebook page, especially if you have a success story as an Extra on a set in Hollywood.

www.Facebook.com/beanextraonvacation

https://twitter.com/touristguide14

www.DarrylDStewart.com

32859555R00070

Made in the USA
Middletown, DE
20 June 2016